AMAZING INVENTIONS

AIRCRAFT

MARY ELIZABETH SALZMANN

Consulting Editor, Diane Craig, M.A./Reading Specialist

Sandcastle

An Imprint of Abdo Publishing
abdopublishing.com

abdopublishing.com

Published by Abdo Publishing, a division of ABDO, PO Box 398166, Minneapolis, Minnesota 55439. Copyright © 2016 by Abdo Consulting Group, Inc. International copyrights reserved in all countries. No part of this book may be reproduced in any form without written permission from the publisher. SandCastle™ is a trademark and logo of Abdo Publishing.

Printed in the United States of America, North Mankato, Minnesota

062015
092015

 THIS BOOK CONTAINS
RECYCLED MATERIALS

Editor: Alex Kuskowski
Content Developer: Nancy Tuminelly
Cover and Interior Design and Production: Mighty Media, Inc.
Photo Credits: Shutterstock

Library of Congress Cataloging-in-Publication Data

Salzmann, Mary Elizabeth, 1968- author.
  Aircraft / Mary Elizabeth Salzmann ; consulting editor, Diane Craig, M.A./Reading Specialist.
    pages cm. -- (Amazing inventions)
  Audience: Grades PreK-3.
  ISBN 978-1-62403-707-8
1. Airplanes--Juvenile literature. 2. Inventions--History--Juvenile literature. [1. Flying machines.]
I. Title.
  TL547.S24 2016
  629.133--dc23
          2014045324

SandCastle™ Level: Transitional

SandCastle™ books are created by a team of professional educators, reading specialists, and content developers around five essential components—phonemic awareness, phonics, vocabulary, text comprehension, and fluency—to assist young readers as they develop reading skills and strategies and increase their general knowledge. All books are written, reviewed, and leveled for guided reading, early reading intervention, and Accelerated Reader™ programs for use in shared, guided, and independent reading and writing activities to support a balanced approach to literacy instruction. The SandCastle™ series has four levels that correspond to early literacy development. The levels are provided to help teachers and parents select appropriate books for young readers.

EMERGING · BEGINNING · TRANSITIONAL · FLUENT

CONTENTS

All About
Aircraft

4

Think
About It

22

Glossary

24

ALL ABOUT AIRCRAFT

There are many kinds of aircraft.

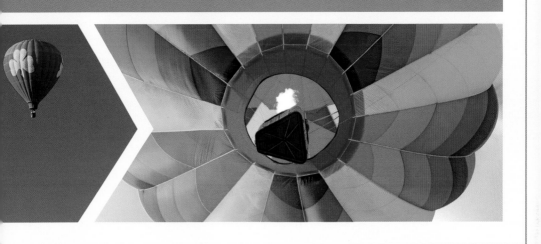

Hot air balloons come in different colors. They can be fun shapes too.

Gliders don't have engines.
The wind holds them up.

The first airplane flew in 1903. It was a **biplane**. Biplanes have two sets of wings.

The air force has fighter jets.
They fly faster than sound.

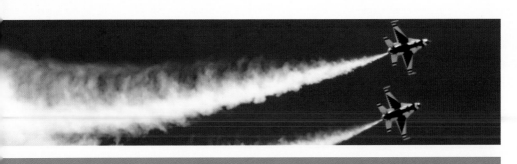

Large airplanes carry
hundreds of people.

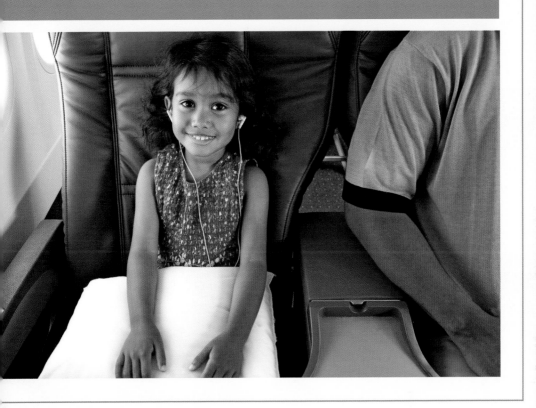

Ashley flies from Texas
to New York.

Some airplanes
can land on water.

Helicopters don't have wings. They have **rotors**.

They take off
straight up.

Rockets go
into space.

The first one was **launched** in 1942.

THINK ABOUT IT

What kind of aircraft would you like to ride in? Where would you go?

23

GLOSSARY

biplane – a kind of airplane that has two sets of wings with one above the other.

glider – an aircraft without an engine.

helicopter – an aircraft with large, rotating blades on top.

launch – to send a spacecraft or missile into space.

rotor – the large blades on a helicopter that turn to lift it into the air.